I'LL TAKE THE PLANE, THE BUS AND THE TRAIN 'TIL I GET THERE!

Travel Book for Kids
Children's Transportation Books

Speedy Publishing LLC
40 E. Main St. #1156
Newark, DE 19711
www.speedypublishing.com

There are several ways to travel around the world, with some getting you to your destination quicker than others and some costing more than others. In this book, we will be learning about the airplane, the bus, and the train.

Airplanes

An airplane, also referred to as an aeroplane or a plane, is a fixed-wing, powered aircraft propelled by the thrust from a propeller or a jet engine. They come in various shapes, sizes, and wing configurations. The many uses for airplanes includes military, recreation, research, and transportation of people and goods.

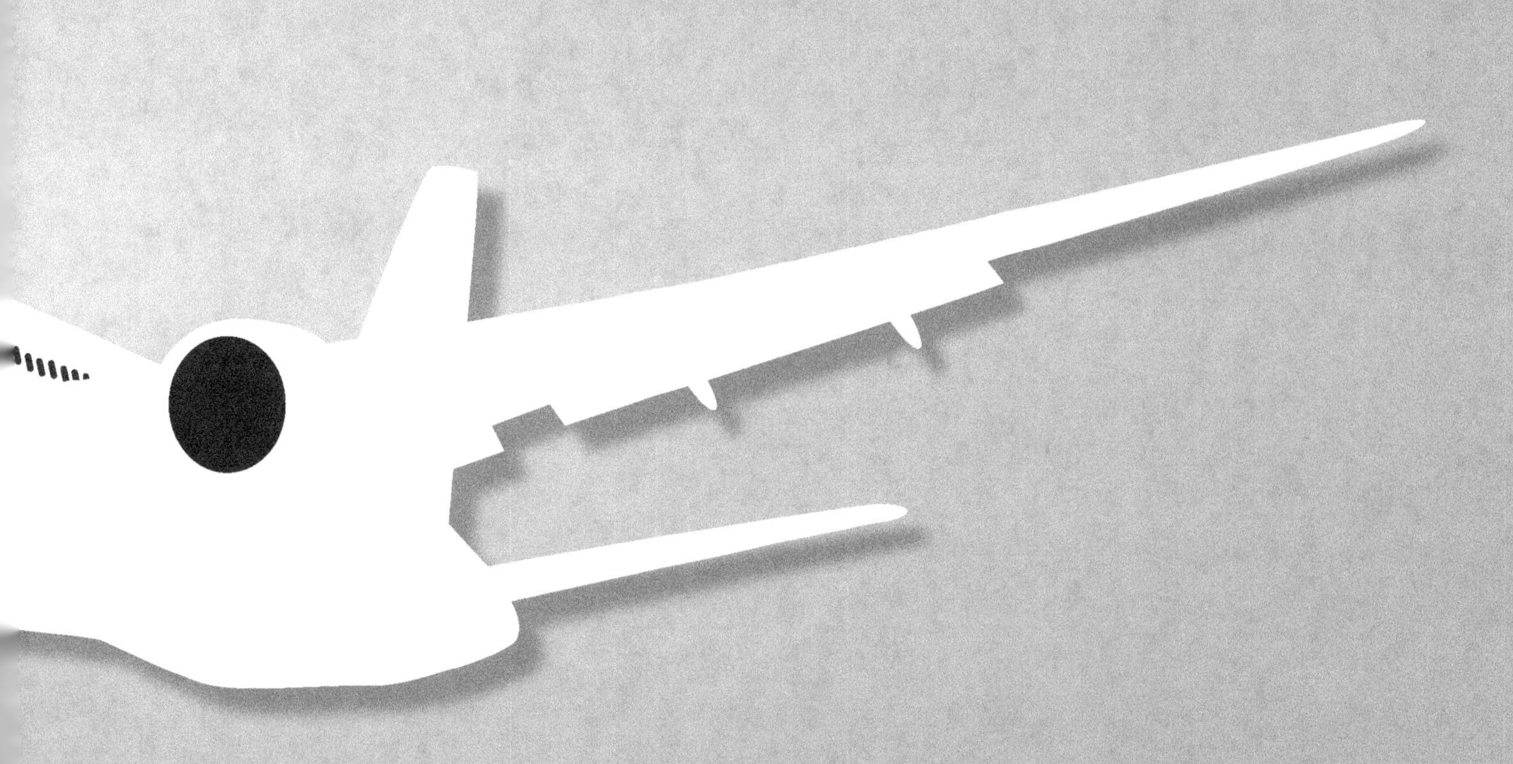

PILOT

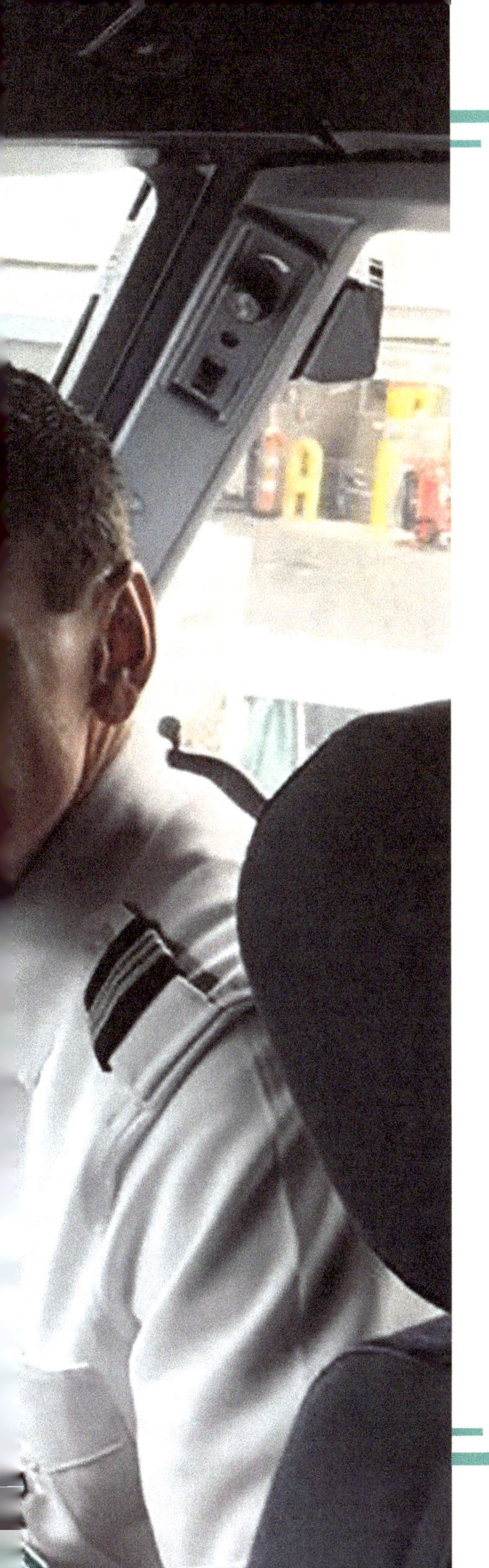

Commercial aviation is a huge industry that involves flying many (tens of thousands) passengers each day. They are mainly flown by a pilot that is on board the plane, but some have been designed to be computer or remotely controlled.

Invention of the Airplane

Wilbur and Orville Wright are credited with the invention of the plane. These brothers were first to succeed in a human flight with an aircraft powered by an engine, but heavier than air, which was a huge milestone and had an impact on transportation around the world.

ORVILLE AND WILBUR WRIGHT

However, it did take time to make it work perfectly and later made it possible for people to travel long distances, taking a lot less time. Trips that would have previously taken days or months by trains and buses, can now be made in only a few hours.

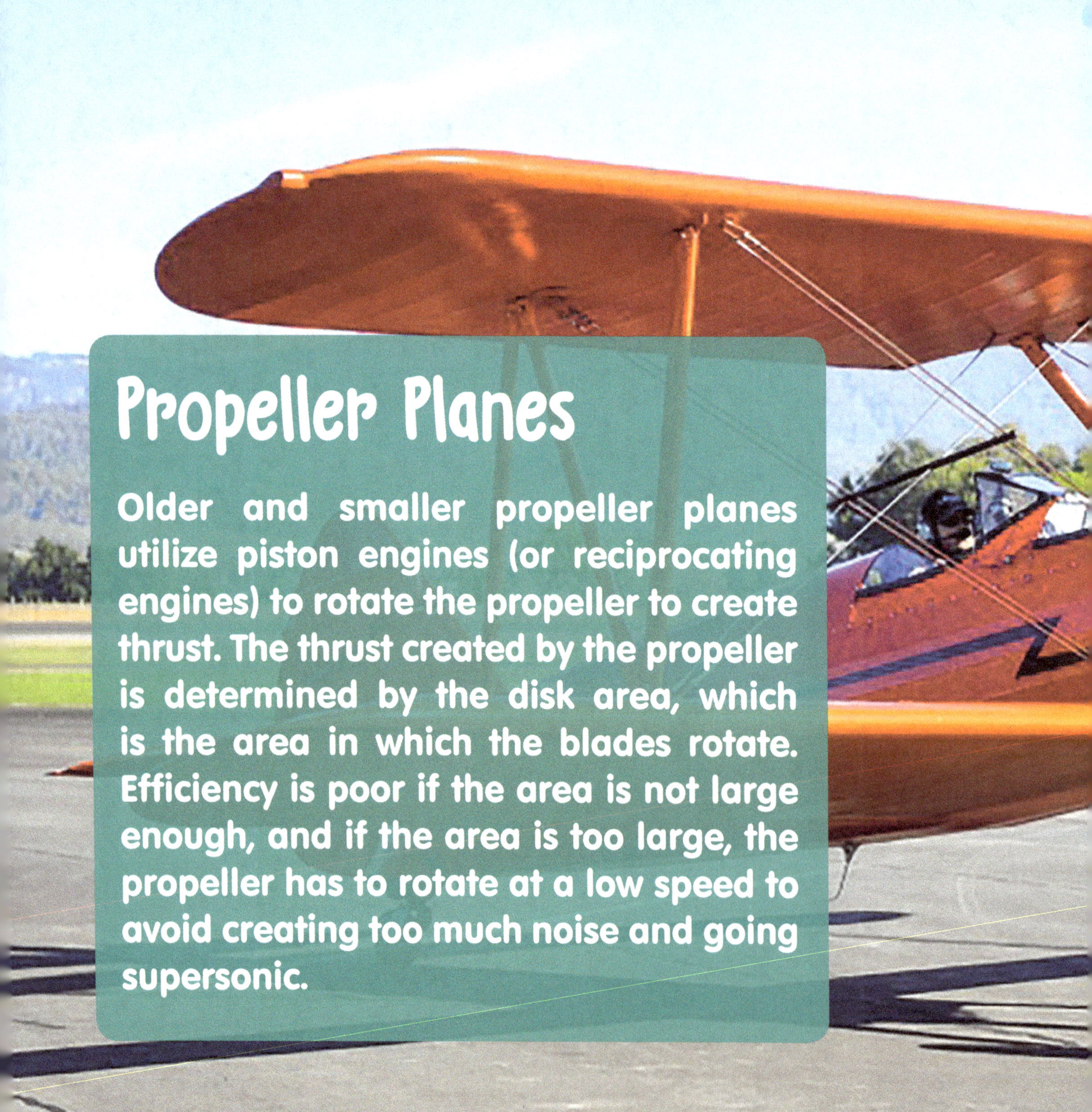

Propeller Planes

Older and smaller propeller planes utilize piston engines (or reciprocating engines) to rotate the propeller to create thrust. The thrust created by the propeller is determined by the disk area, which is the area in which the blades rotate. Efficiency is poor if the area is not large enough, and if the area is too large, the propeller has to rotate at a low speed to avoid creating too much noise and going supersonic.

CESSNA 172

Due to this limitation, planes that travel below mach .5 favor propellers, and jets are a better option at a higher speed. Propeller engines cost less to purchase and maintain and often are quieter and remain the common choice for light aviation aircraft, similar to the Cessna 172.

Jet Engine Planes

Jet aircraft use jet engines since the limitations of the propellers are not a factor for jet propulsion. The jet engines are a lot more powerful and are relatively quiet and they work well at higher altitudes. Modern jet planes mostly use turbofan jet engines which balances the advantages of using a propeller, but retaining the power and exhaust speed of a jet.

B

Electric Engine Planes

The electric aircraft is run on electric motors rather than an internal combustion engine, and the electricity comes from solar cells, fuel cells, power beaming, ultracapacitors, or batteries. The electric aircraft are currently experimental, including manned and unmanned aircraft, but some models are already on the market.

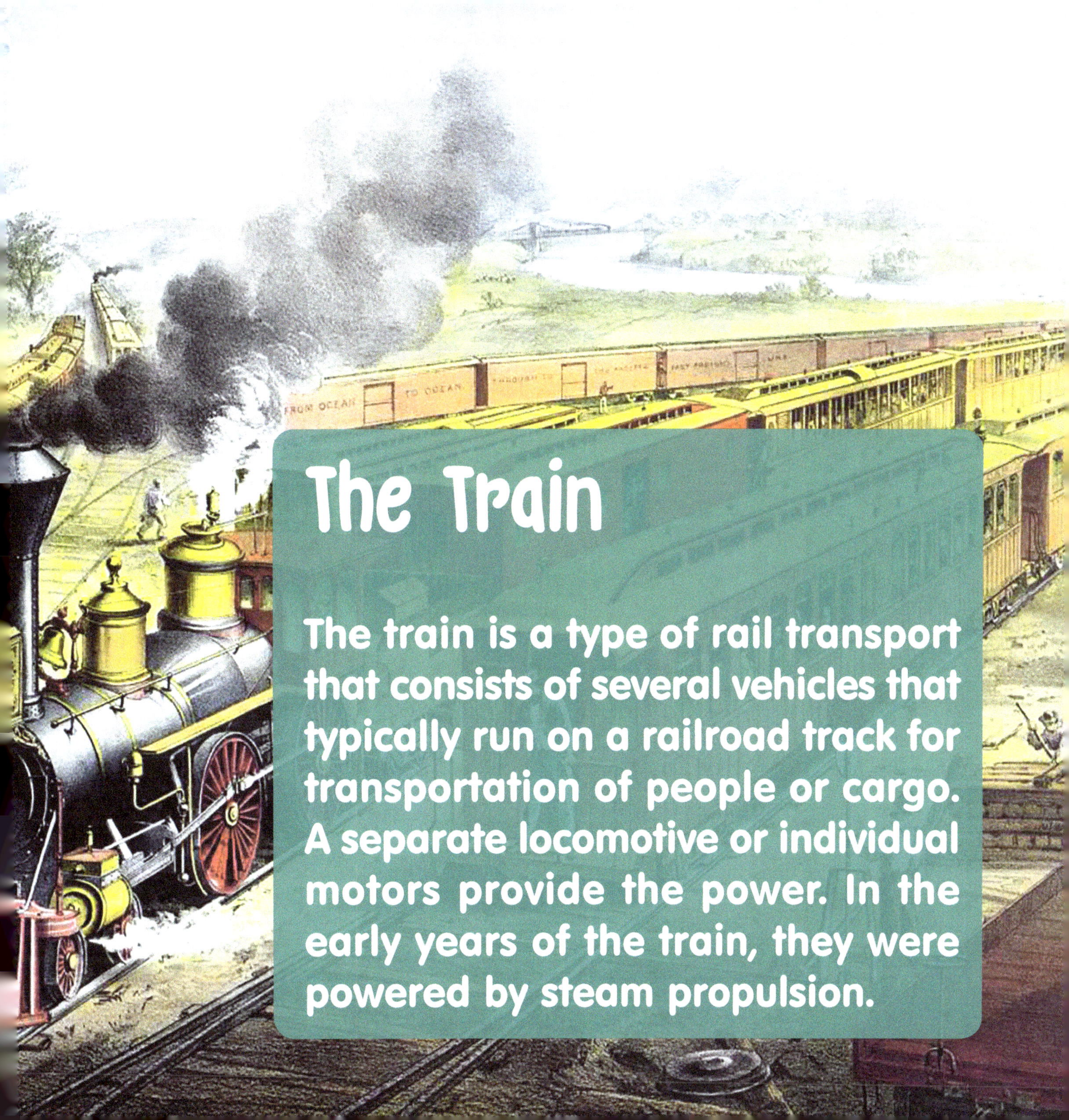

The Train

The train is a type of rail transport that consists of several vehicles that typically run on a railroad track for transportation of people or cargo. A separate locomotive or individual motors provide the power. In the early years of the train, they were powered by steam propulsion.

MODERN TRAIN

The modern rail forms are electric and diesel locomotives. Other sources of energy have included horses, gravity, water or engine-driven rope or wire, batteries, pneumatics, as well as gas turbines. The railroad tracks typically consist of two rails, occasionally supplemented with an additional rail such as rack rails and electric conducting rails.

There are different types of trains that are created for certain purposes. It may consist of one or more locomotives and the attached railroad cars, or a multiple unit that is self-propelled. The original trains were pulled by horses, gravity powered, or hauled by ropes. Starting in the early 19th century, most were being powered by steam.

Р.У. ж.д. У.127

Beginning in the 1910s, the diesel locomotives and the electric locomotives started replacing the steam engines, as the newer trains were cleaner and less labor-intensive. However, they were more expensive and complex. At around the same time, the self-propelled vehicles became more popular for passenger service.

Passenger Trains

A passenger train carries passengers in vehicles that are usually fast and long. The high-speed rail is one of the more notable and growing long-distance categories for carrying passengers. Innovate Maglex technology has for years been worked on to reach a speed over 310 mph (500 km/h). In the United Kingdom, as well as in most other countries, the difference between a railway and a tramway is precise and is defined by law.

TRAMWAY

Passenger trains must provide head-end power for each coach to be used for heating and lighting, which is not required for freight trains. This power can come directly from the locomotive's prime mover, or from a diesel generator that provides power in the coaches. On routes where head-end-equipped locomotives might not be available, a generator can be used.

PASSENGER TRAIN

The conductor oversees the passenger train. They are typically assisted by additional crew members, such as porters or service attendants. Earlier train travel crews would include two conductors; the train conductor referenced previously as well as a Pullman conductor, who was in charge of sleeping car personnel.

CONDUCTOR

Some of the passenger trains use double-decker (bi-level) cars which can carry additional passengers in each coach. The safety of passenger trains has evolved dramatically over time, and travel by train is extremely safe.

8269
8269
BNSF
8269
ES44CA

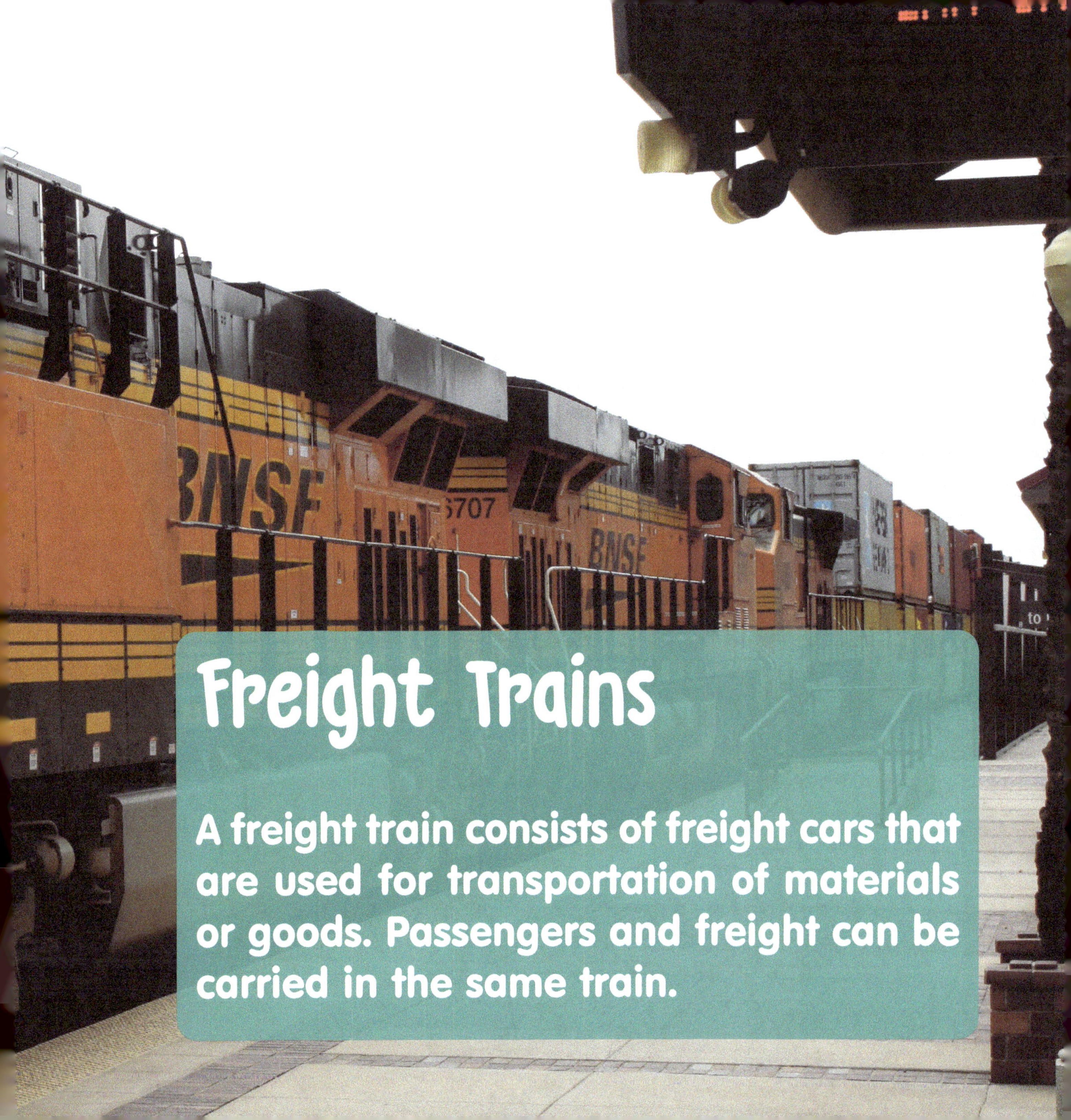

Freight Trains

A freight train consists of freight cars that are used for transportation of materials or goods. Passengers and freight can be carried in the same train.

SCHOOL BUS
ROUTE
5076
SAF-T-LINER
STOP
0702

Buses

A bus is a vehicle for the road that is intended to carry multiple passengers, some can carry as many as 300 passengers. The single-decker rigid bus is the most common bus. Double-decker buses and articulated buses are designed to carry larger loads and minibuses and midibuses are used to transport loads. Coach buses are used to travel longer distances. City buses will usually charge a fare for the ride, but there is no charge to ride a school bus.

740
carousel
link
874
AE61 EWP

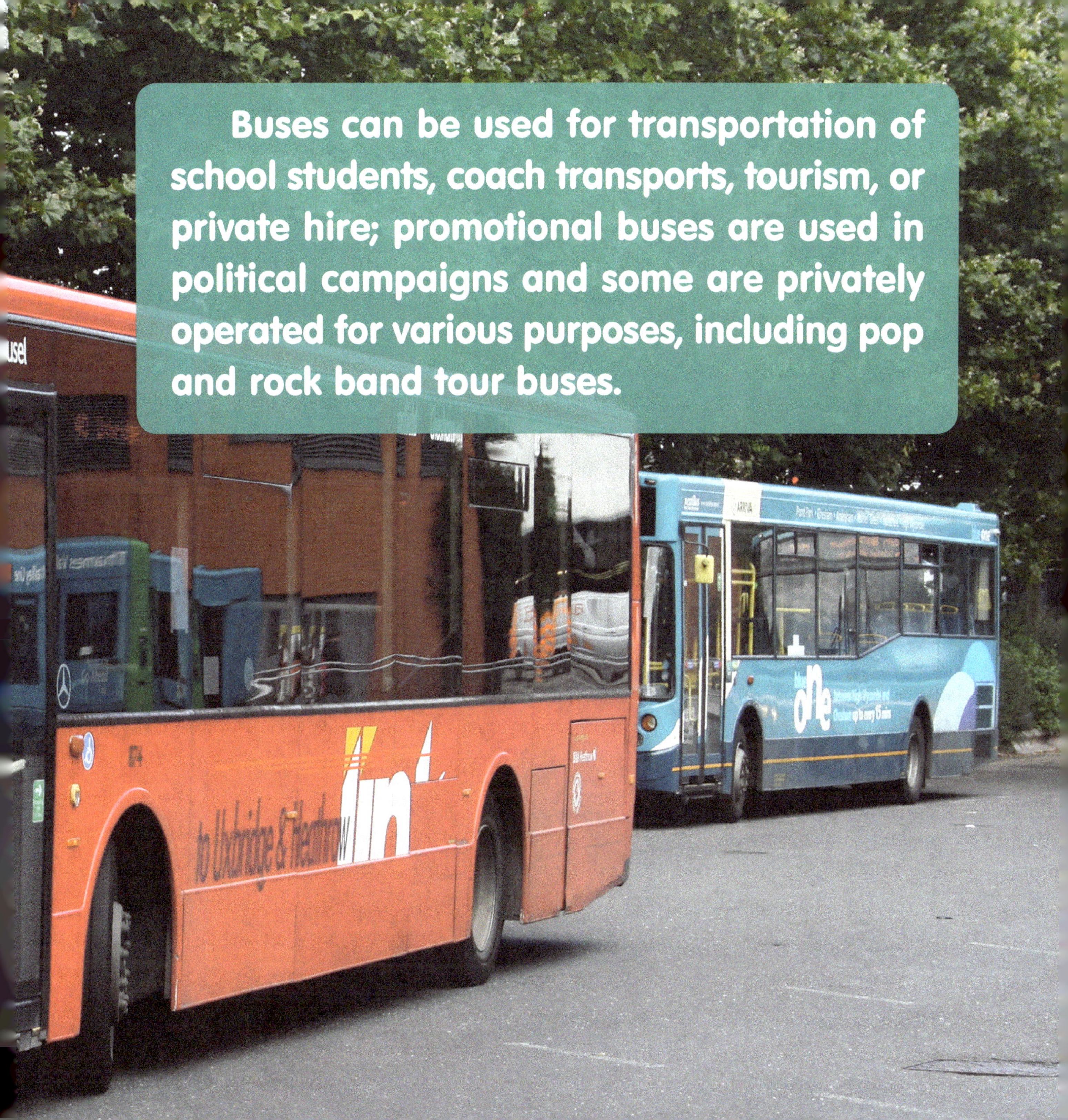

Buses can be used for transportation of school students, coach transports, tourism, or private hire; promotional buses are used in political campaigns and some are privately operated for various purposes, including pop and rock band tour buses.

ELECTRIC BUS

The beginning of the bus started with horse-drawn buses in the 1820s, steam buses in the 1830s; and followed in 1882 by the electric trolleybuses. In 1895, the bus became powered by the internal combustion engine, also known as the motor bus. Interest has been recently growing in electric buses, fuel cell buses, hybrid electric buses, and buses powered by biodiesel, which uses compressed natural gas. Bus manufacturing has become increasingly globalized as of the 2010s, with the same bus designs being used around the world.

Steam Buses

Pioneered in the 1830s in England, thanks to Walter Hancock and by associates of Sir Goldsworthy Gurney, the steam power buses became necessary to provide transportation for road conditions that were too dangerous for horse-drawn transportation.

GOLDSWORTHY GURNEY

STEAM CARRIAGE

On April 22, 1833, the original mechanically propelled omnibus hit the streets of London. The steam carriages travelled faster than the horse-drawn carriage, they were less likely to turn over, they were cheaper to run, and because of their wide tires they caused less road damage.

17 DOWNTOWN
2214
To Buses

Trolleybuses

The electric trolleybus works by using trolley poles that are fed to overhead wires. The trolleybus was developed by the Siemans brothers, Ernst Werner in Germany and William in England.

DR. ERNST WERNER VON SIEMENS

The Electromote, the first trolleybus, was created by Dr. Ernst Werner von Siemens and presented in Halensee, Germany in 1882. While this experimental vehicle fulfilled the technical criteria of the trolleybus, they dismantled it after the demonstration.

In 1901, near Dresden, Germany, Max Schiemann started a trolleybus that carried passengers. Even though it only operated until 1904, he had developed the bus that we now know as the standard trolleybus current collection system. On June 20, 1911, Bradford and Leeds were the first two cities in Great Britain to put these trolleybuses into service.

2

MA HT 600

Motor Buses

In 1895, two passenger bus lines operated for a short time in Siegerland, Germany, but were not profitable. They used a six-passenger motor carriage that had been designed from the 1893 Benz Viktoria. In 1898, another commercial bus line used the same model for a brief time in the rural area that surrounded Llandudno, Wales.

During the 20th century, models expanded, which led to the introduction of full-sized, contemporary recognizable, full-sized buses from the 1950s. Designed in the 1950s, the AEC Routemaster became a pioneering design and is still a London icon today. Its innovative design utilized lightweight aluminum and techniques that were developed during World War II in production of aircraft. Also introduced was the independent front suspension, a totally automatic gearbox, power steering, and power-hydraulic braking.

Shepherds Bush
220
TOOTING STN
EGP 1J
11
Fulham Chelsea
Victoria Charing +
Fleet Street Bank
SLOANE SQUARE
737 DYE

Depending on how much time you have or how much money you want to spend, these are only three of the options available to get to where you like to go. If you want to get there quickly, you might want to take the plane. Maybe it might be fun to take the train. Or, you may want to spend less money and take less time and travel by bus.

For additional information about these three modes of transportation, or additional methods of transportation you can visit your local library, research the internet, or ask question of your teachers, family and friends.

Visit

www.BabyProfessorBooks.com

to download Free Baby Professor eBooks and view our catalog of new and exciting Children's Books

www.ingramcontent.com/pod-product-compliance
Lightning Source LLC
LaVergne TN
LVHW060828170826
845678LV00010B/1923

9798869435460